1 MONTH OF
FREE
READING

at

www.ForgottenBooks.com

By purchasing this book you are
eligible for one month membership to
ForgottenBooks.com, giving you
unlimited access to our entire
collection of over 1,000,000 titles via
our web site and mobile apps.

To claim your free month visit:
www.forgottenbooks.com/free423857

ISBN 978-0-656-17969-5
PIBN 10423857

This book is a reproduction of an important historical work. Forgotten Books uses
state-of-the-art technology to digitally reconstruct the work, preserving the original format
whilst repairing imperfections present in the aged copy. In rare cases, an imperfection in
the original, such as a blemish or missing page, may be replicated in our edition. We do,
however, repair the vast majority of imperfections successfully; any imperfections that
remain are intentionally left to preserve the state of such historical works.

HE MERITS

—OF—

OME RULE"

—IN—

RELAND,

BY

SEPH NIMMO, Jr.

"THE LONG-ISLANDER" Print 1886.

The Merits of "Home Rule" in Ireland.

Mr. Gladstone's appeal to the people of Great Britain and Ireland has been made, and the reform of Home Rule, although not fully endorsed at the polls, has yet advanced to a stage at which final success appears to be inevitable. Since the result of the struggle has been made known, the criticism has been freely offered, both in this country and in England, that the great Premier has been precipitate, that he had better have postponed the election until the autumn, for the reason that the English mind is slow to adopt new political dogmas. This appears to be the philosophy of people who have little cause for pride of foresight, but who take infinite delight in the infallibility of their backsight. The world, however, recognizes the fact that Mr. Gladstone is not only a statesman of great resources, but also a politician of wonderful astuteness. No man knows better than he that the political advancement of nations proceeds not like the steady flowing river, but like the receding and advancing billows of the incoming tide. At the beginning, Mr. Gladstone announced his purpose of forcing the consideration of his

Home Rule Measure upon Parliament, to the
exclusion of all other legislation except the
passage of bills for providing the means of
carrying on the government. Accordingly
he demanded for its discussion five out of six
days of each week, a right exercised by the
ministry only in cases of emergency. The
election so soon following the final vote in
Parliament was clearly a part of the same line
of tactics employed in the House of Commons. His uniform declarations from the
beginning have been to the effect that he
should regard defeat in Parliament and at
the polls as merely incidents in a struggle
the result of which must be the eventual tri-
umph of the principle announced in the
Home Rule Bill. He has succeeded in making the measure the foremost and absorbing
political issue of Great Britain, and all the
advices indicate that no other measure can
command the attention of the country until
this is disposed of.

The present time appears to be opportune
for presenting an analysis and explanation
of the features of the bill, which I am able to
do, having received a copy of it at the hands
of a friend, from the Hon. Wm. J. Lane,
member of Parliament for the City of Cork.

Generally it has been said that the
Home Rule Bill proposes to confer rights
f local government similar to our state gov-

ernments. But that is not sufficiently accurate in order to convey a definite idea of the merits of the measure. The rights granted are in fact much narrower and more constrained the powers of government enjoyed by the states of this country, as will appear from the following review:

THE LEGISLATIVE AUTHORITY.

The legislative authority proposed to be created in Ireland is summarily described in the Bill in these words, "There shall be established in Ireland a Legislature consisting of Her Majesty, the Queen, and an Irish Legislative Body." In a word the Lord Lieutenant of Ireland, appointed by the Crown, and paid out of the Royal Exchequer, "shall give or withold the assent of Her Majesty to Bills passed by the Irish Parliament." This legislative body is debarred from passing laws in regard to the status or dignity of the crown, the making of war or peace, the army or navy, forts or arsenals, intercourse with foreign countries, dignities or titles of honor; treason, alienage or naturalization; the postal or telegraph service; navigation, beacons or lighthouses; money; copyright, or patent rights. Nor shall the Irish Legislature make any law respecting an establish ment or endowment of religion, or prohibiting the free exercise thereof, or in any manner working disability on account of religious belief, or in any manner prejudicially affecting the right to establish or maintain denominational schools. The Irish Parliament is to consist of two branches known as "The first and the second order." The first order is to consist of one hundred and three members, of whom seventy-five are to be elective, and twenty-eight peerage members and the second order is to consist of two hundred and four elective members. A property qualification is established with the limit of two hundred pounds a year; income, or a capital value of four thousand pounds.

Whether Ireland shall or shall not continue to send members to the Imperial Parliament to legislate upon matters other than those relating to Ireland is as yet an open question. In fact Mr. Gladstone has repeatedly declared the entire detail of the Bill to be subject to amendment or even to radical change. His present fight is directed to the single thought of establishing the principle of the bill, viz. : the right of Ireland to manage her own internal affairs.

THE EXECUTIVE AUTHORITY.

The Lord Lieutenant, who is to be the Chief Executive of Ireland, is to be appointed by the Queen ; his salary, and the expenses of his household and establishment to be paid from the Royal Exchequer, and the Legislature of Ireland is debarred from passing any Act relating to his office or functions.

The veto power over legislation by the Irish
Parliament is delegated to him, subject to
instructions which may from time to time be
given him by Her Majesty. He is also em-
powered to exercise the prerogatives of Her
Majesty in respect to summoning, prorogu-
ing and dissolving the Irish Legislative
Body. It must be remembered that this, to
us Americans, apparently despotic power is
so exercised in Great Britain, as to voice
public sentiment even more promptly than it
finds expression in this country through the
election of a House of Representatives once
in two years.

THE JUDICIARY.

Under the provision of the Home Rule
Bill, the Judges of the Supreme Court of
Judicature, and other Supreme Courts of Ireland and of County Courts, and of other
courts of like jurisdiction in Ireland, will continue to be appointable by the crown, and to
be removable in pursuance of an address to
Her Majesty from both branches of the Irish
Legislative Body. The salaries of such offi-
cers will be paid out of the "Consolidated
Fund of the United Kingdom."

OTHER FEATURES OF THE HOME RULE BILL.

Constitutional questions arising in the
course of Irish legislation are to be decided
by appeal to Her Majesty in Council. This
in the eyes of Americans involves the anom

aly of placing the decision of questions
of a legal and judicial nature in the deter-
mination of a body which from its constitution is moved by political rather than by
judicial considerations.

Evidently the legislative, executive, and
judicial power granted to the proposed Irish
government by Mr. Gladstone's bill, constitute a scheme of government very much in-
ferior in scope and function to that very gen-
eral and unconstrained provision of our national constitution which provides for the admis-
sion of new states into the Union upon the
simple condition that they shall have a government which is republican in form.

FINANCE.

The system of finance provided in the Home
Rule Bill. appears in the light of our own national experiences to be not only clumsy, but
unnecessarily complex. Under its provisions Ireland is to collect all internal taxes,
and to pay a portion over to the Consolidated Fund of the United Kingdom. In case
of war the bill, in terms, makes it necessary
for the imperial government to call upon Ireland for its financial contingent. This is
the method of finance which prevailed in
this country from Nov. 18, 1777 to April
30, 1879, when the present Federal Union
went into operation. The evils of the old
system of finance constituted one of the rea-

sons for establishing "a more perfect Union."
Our present system of national finance which
was organized by Alexander Hamilton, is
entirely independent of state interference.
It has saved the country a world of trouble,
especially during the late war, and in the
adjustment and payment of the national
debt.

OBJECTIONS TO THE HOME RULE BILL.

The opponents of the Home Rule Bill
have during the recent campaign repeatedly
declared that the Parnellites intend to use
their new powers to enable them to set up an
independent government. This however can
only be regarded as a political libel. Mr.
Parnell and his coadjutors in the new movement indignantly repel the charge. Long
ago, Lord Macaulay exposed the absurdity
of the assumption that any political party
can entertain secret designs or cherish pur-
poses ulterior to those which it professes.
But the disingenuousness of the objection is
evident from the fact that under the Home
Rule Bill, the imperial government retains
its absolute control of the Army and Navy,
and of all forts, arsenals and munitions of
war, and that it will in no manner be in a
less favorable position to suppress insurrection in Ireland, than at the present time,
conditions governing the settlement of the
Irish question.

The conditions surrounding and governing the settlement of the Irish question are so widely different from those which prevail in this country that it is well nigh impossible for an American to comprehend, much less to explain the considerations involved in the details of the Home Rule Bill. The social and political institutions of Great Britain and Ireland are characterized by peculiarities which have no correspondent whatever in the political institutions of this country. I refer especially to ecclesiasticism in politics, to inherited religious prejudices, to the moral influence of historical events in the course of the developement of the country, to the influence of class distinctions, in social and political affairs and especially the institution of a hereditary nobility, to the nature and extent of landed proprietorships and their relation to the agricultural classes, to the law of primogeniture and entail, and to the incidents of a monarchy cherished by a people who in the detail of their governmental system have in certain particulars taken hold on democratic ideas even more vigorously than ourselves.

But the whole course of the development of political idea in Europe and in America has proceded from diametrically opposite points. Our system is in fact the very invert of theirs. We began our political existence with only "Home Rule." It is no stretch of

the verities of our political history to assert
that the town was the germ of government
in this country. Mr. Charles R. Street of
this village has in his interesting historical
sketch of Huntington shown that it was at
one time a governmental autonomy. At the
time of the Declaration of Independence governmental sovereignty existed only in the
states, but in the course of events, they were
forced by the exigencies of self preservation,
and the highest considerations of self interest
to evolve the national sovereignty which since
1789 has constituted us a nation. Neverthe-
less, the state now touches the individual at
a hundred points where the national government touches him at one, and the tendency
toward sending the exercise of governmental
powers to the extremities is stronger than
that toward increasing the powers of the government at Washington. These two tenden-
cies are not conflicting but co-ordinate. Both
tend to functional efficiency in administration.
The constitution of our own state now con-
fers upon the boards of supervisors of the
several counties, certain "powers of local
legislation and administration," and as we all
know this special form of "home rule" has
operated beneficially for Long Island particu-
larly, in respect to its fisheries, which interests it has in common with no other part of
the state.

But the relation of political institutions to
the people is widely different in Great Britain, and in fact throughout Europe. There
the theory has from time immemorial taken
possession of the minds of men, that the germ
of political power resides in the national sovereignty, and that all local self government
and in fact all popular liberty has, in the pro-
gress of civilization and of reform in gov
ernmental methods been accorded by, or
w rested from the sovereign power.

IRELAND'S GRIEVANCES.

During the recent debates in Parliament
and in the campaign just closed, Mr. Gladstone has labored to impress upon his coun
trymen the advantages of federated gover
mental powers, and the idea that the empire
would be all the stronger for local self goverment. This idea as before shown is elemen-
tary to our system of goverment. It is
therefore quite incomprehensible to us that
so large a proportion of the British nation is
not to-day educated up to the doctrine that
the summation and formulated expression of
all the liberties which a people can, and ought
to enjoy under the guardianship of legal
sanction, is a code of laws framed with a
view to meeting their specific wants, and con-
formed to their specific experiences and the
particular conditions which constitute their
environment, and that such laws can only be

devised by those whose interest it is to have
them enacted. The sullen answer of Tory
and Conservative to Mr. Gladstone's eloquent,
and almost pathetic pleadings upon this point
is that he is "taking a step toward the dis-
memberment of the empire". They also
point to the fact that Ireland has already
been granted many important concessions,
and, that she is unreasonable now in asking for
more. But all experience proves that a
proud people can never be satisfied to barter
rights for privileges. A surfeit of largesses
may be heaped upon them but they will bate
the donor, who at the same time deprives
them of a single liberty. When therefore
John Bright, refers to the enfranchisement
of Catholics, the disestablishment of_the
church-state in Ireland, the reform of the
land laws, the arrears act, and other legisla
tion. ending last year with an act securing
the widest household sufferage, and asks
"Could any government in the same length
of time have done more for any people", we
are prompted to refer him for reply, to the
noble and statesmanlike utterance of Cardinal Manning in his recent letter to an Amer
ican friend ; "In your majestic union there
is a central power which binds all your liberties and legislatures into one commonwealth.
England, Ireland and Scotland must, in my
belief, all alike have home rule in affairs that
are not imperial ; but there is an august sov-

ereignty of a thousand years, the centre of a world-wide empire standing in the midst of us.——— — ———————The sovereignty pervades all its parts and will ever restrain and promptly redress all excesses of delegated power."

But there is undoubtedly an expression less specious than that above mentioned to allowing Ireland the advantages of "Home Rule." It is an objection heard only in deep under tones. The lesson of the revolt of her American colonies, gradually forced Great Britian to accord to her remaining colonies commercial independence. By virtue of such privileges, the colonies generally have discarded the sophisms of free trade, and have enacted tariffs protective of their own manufacturing and other industries. The real bugbear of "Home Rule" at the present time appears therefore to be, that Ireland might in time gain the right to make her own tariff, in which case she would in all probability discriminate against Mr. John Bright's Birmingham carpets, and against many other products of English manufacture. So hidden away under much inconsequential rubbish may be found a very concrete objection expressed in terms of pounds, shillings and pence.

It is of course impossible in a single newspaper article to portray the wrongs of Ire-

land. They had their origin centuries ago,
in the conflicts of antagonistic races, and in
religious differences. From the time when
the Briton first dominated Ireland she has
been held by military force. In referring to
the period of reconstruction involved in plac
ing the Scottish King, James VI, upon the
English throne as James I, Lord Macaulay
says "Ireland was undisguisedly governed as
a dependency won by the sword." Since that
time she has suffered woes which would have
obliterated a people less brave and less ro-
bust. On the first day of the present century the Irish Parliment was abrogated and
the so-called "Union" was inaugurated under circumstances of outrage and perfidy.
For twenty nine years thereafter, Catholics
were disfranchised through what Mr. Gladstone in a recent speech in Parliament has
declared to be "a woeful disregard of solemn
promises." Finally, in the year 1829, Catholic emancipation was achieved, mainly
through the eloquent pleadings of Daniel
O'Connell. But as Mr. Gladstone observes,
this right was accorded, "not from good-will
but from abject terror, and to avoid civil
war."

The most aggravating evil, which for near
ly two centuries afflicted the Irish people,
Catholics and Presbyterians alike, and which
nurtured their animosity toward England,
was the fact that they were taxed for the

support of a state-church with which they held no voluntary connection, and for which they had no affection. This abuse was finally abolished in the year 1871 under the leadership of Mr. Gladstone.

Perhaps the most serious cause of complaint by the Irish people has arisen from the failure of the Imperial Parliament to act upon Irish interests. Failure to act is oftentimes a deed done, for time legislates as well as parliaments, and the decree *too late*, stands as the finality of many a political opportunity lost. In this country, with a Congress charged only with the duty of attending to national affairs, there are many important bills which die at the expiration of each Congress. How then must it be in the case of a Parliament charged with the duty of legislating for an Empire upon which the sun never sets, and also with the home interests of England, Scotland and Ireland. Even in the legislation which is effected blunders are made from sheer ignorance of Irish affairs. But Irish interest suffer far more from inattention.

Besides the evils of governmental mismanagement, Ireland has suffered untold miseries from her system of land tenures, which cry aloud for reform Absentee landordism has added the coldness of neglect to the hardships of a system, harsh enough in its legal characteristics. Small wonder is it that Ireland has for more than a hundred years presented a scene of domestic turbulence and of downright violence. Since the beginning of the present century the writ of *Habeas Corpus* has been suspended twenty four times, and various bills have been passed by Parliament for the purpose of suppressing insurrection and of preventing threatened outbreak. In his closing speech of the recent debate in the House of Commons, Mr. Parnell said "During the last five years you have had suspension of the *Habeas Corpus* in Ireland A thousand of your fellow—subjects have been imprisoned without specific charge, many for long periods,—twenty months,—without trial, and without any intention to try them. You have had the right of domicile infringed at all hours of the day and night; You have fined the innocent for the guilty : You have assumed the power to expel aliens from the country, you have renewed the "Curfew law" and "blood money" of your Norman Conquerors ; you have gagged the press, seized and suppressed newspapers, manufactured new crimes and offenses. - - - - - - - - - - - - - - and if the proposed coercion policy, which is involved in the rejection of this bill is to be carried out,—all this and much more you will do again." On the same occasion Mr. Gladstone declared the treat.

ment of Ireland to be "a black blot upon the pages of England's history."

WHAT "HOME RULE" OFFERS.

The provisions of the Home Rule Bill have already been described. Unquestionably the degree of favor with which it has been received in England and in Scotland is due very largely to Mr. Gladstone's personal influence. Without going into the detail of the benefits likely to be afforded by the bill, for that would transcend the proper limits of this article, it is sufficient, here to give Mr. Parnell's opinion of its merits. In his closing speech in the House of Commons he said: —"The Irish people can accept this bill; they have accepted it without reserve, as a measure which may be considered the final settlement of the whole question." But as a practical measure of adjusting political differences, the chief value of the Home Rule Bill consists in the moral influence of the circumstances under which it has been proposed, and under which, with the preserved life of Mr, Gladstone the principle which it announces will in all probability be enacted into law. Unlike other measures of reform which have come to the Irish people as trophies of a conflict, and for that reason have buried no resentments, this comes to them in the manly spirit of good fellowship, with stalwart honesty of faith in them, and hope

for them, and charity toward them. It is at
once an act of justice and a becoming appeal
to a race characterized by warm hearts as
well as strong heads. In the finest sense it
is a measure of Union. There is about It
"the touch of nature" which "makes the
whole world kin." Happily too it comes at
a time when the Irish people, Catholic and
Protestants,—are united in purpose and in
organization. The most benign feature of
the whole movement consists in the fact that
although the Catholic population of Ireland
largely preponderates, leadership is now without rivalry accorded to Charles Stewart Parnell, a Presbyterian. The import of this fact
may be the better comprehended by stating
that of the total number of church adherents in
Ireland in 1881 there were 3,951,888 Catholics, 485,503 Presbyterians, 635,670 fol-
lowers of the Church of England, and 97.778
adherents of all other religious denomina
tions.

But this is not the first time that Irish
Catholics have followed the lead of Protestants, in their attempts to throw off the yoke
of political oppression. There were Dean
Swift, and Theobald Wolfe Tone, and Rob
ert Emmet and Edward Fitzgerald, and
Henry Grattan and many others of less celeb
rity. Could the Catholics of Ireland give a
better pledge of their sincerity, or a more
convincing proof of their honesty of purpose.

It is a cruel aspersion upon a chivalric race to assume now that they will prostitute civil liberty to the cause of religious intolerance.

Nothwithstanding the efforts of Tory leaders to sow the seeds of political dissension, and to excite religious strife between Catholies and Protestants, the Home Rule Bill has been accepted by all true Irishmen without regard to creed. From Westminster, Cardinal Manning sends his hearty endorsement of the bill, and unstinted commendation of Mr. Parnell, and from Princeton, the Rev. Doctor Mc Cosh. President of the College of New Jersey, who may be regarded as the representative Protestant Irishman in America expresses his warm sympathy in, and adhesion to Mr. Gladstone's measure of relief for his native isle. Cardinal Manning, and Doctor McCosh both accept it, as being purely political in its character, and as an act of justice to an oppressed people.

No movement in Europe, during the present century has so strongly elicited the attention or evoked the sympathy of the people of this country, nor has there been presented to them a spectacle so fascinating as the action of England's greatest stateman, who after a career of unexampled success in devising and promoting measures of political reform, now in the fullness of his fame, and at a period

of life, reaching almost to the ultimate limits of the allotted time of man upon earth, implores his countrymen, in the treatment of a portion of their fellow subjects, to substitute love for hate, trust for suspicion, generosity for selfishness, respect for contempt, and justice for oppression, and who in the joyous anticipation of the dawn of a brighter day for his country, exclaims with all the ardor of youth—"Ring out the old, ring in the new."

JOSEPH NIMMO, Jr.

Huntington, N. Y., July 16th, 1886.

CPSIA information can be obtained
at www.ICGtesting.com
Printed in the USA
BVHW04*1419030818
523478BV00007B/28/P